Welcome the Stranger Among Us

UNITY
IN
Diversity

A STATEMENT OF THE U.S. CATHOLIC BISHOPS
UNITED STATES CONFERENCE OF CATHOLIC BISHOPS • WASHINGTON, D.C.

The pastoral statement *Welcoming the Stranger Among Us: Unity in Diversity* was developed by the National Conference of Catholic Bishops' Committee on Migration. It was approved by the full body of bishops at their November 2000 general meeting as a statement of the National Conference of Catholic Bishops and is authorized for publication by the undersigned.

Msgr. Dennis M. Schnurr
General Secretary, NCCB/USCC

Photographs: Cover—Cathy Joyce (upper right), PhotoDisc™ (lower right, upper left), EyeWire™ (lower left). Inside—CNS/*L'Osservatore Romano*, p. iv; USCCB/Eric Brooks Photography, p. 6; CNS/Michael Alexander, pp. 9, 12; Michael Hoyt, pp. 14, 22, 29, 44; Refugee Resettlement Program, Diocese of Fort Wayne-South Bend, p. 36; Chris Duffey, p. 38; Cathy Joyce, p. 47; Catholic Community Services, Newark, N.J., p. 50; Mileva Losic, p. 57.

Excerpts from *Vatican II: The Conciliar and Post Conciliar Documents, New Revised Edition*, edited by Austin Flannery, OP, copyright © 1996, Costello Publishing Company, Inc., Northport, N.Y., are used with permission of the publisher. All rights reserved.

Scripture text used in this work are taken from the *New American Bible*, copyright © 1991, 1986, and 1970 by the Confraternity of Christian Doctrine, Washington, D.C. 20017 and are used with permission of the copyright owner. All rights reserved.

First Printing, November 2000
Second Printing, October 2001

ISBN 1-57455-375-5

Copyright © 2000, United States Conference of Catholic Bishops, Inc., Washington, D.C. All rights reserved. No part of this work may be reproduced or transmitted in any form or by any means, electronic or mechanical, including photocopying, recording, or by any information storage and retrieval system, without permission in writing from the copyright holder.

CONTENTS

SUMMARY

O
n June 2, 2000, the Jubilee Day for Migrants and Refugees, Pope John Paul II celebrated the Eucharist in St. Peter's Square for over 50,000 migrants, refugees, people on the move, and their chaplains from all over the world. The Eucharist drew that great diversity of people into unity in the communion of Father, Son, and Holy Spirit, realizing a Jubilee Year hope for the Church: "to gather into one the dispersed children of God," "to sum up all things in Christ, in heaven and on earth" (Jn 11:52; Eph 1:10).

Unity in diversity is the vision that we bishops, as pastors of the Church in the United States, offer to our people as they welcome the new immigrants and refugees who come to our shores. In the past thirty-five years the number and variety of immigrants coming to the United States have provided a great challenge for us as pastors. Previous immigrants had come predominantly from Europe or as slaves from Africa, but many of the new immigrants come from Latin America and the Caribbean, Asia and the Pacific Islands, the Middle East, Africa, Eastern Europe, and the former Soviet Union and Yugoslavia. Though a good number come as skilled workers and professionals, the greater number come as refugees and immigrants on the edge of survival; large numbers join families already here; others arrive without proper documents. Many were forced to leave their homeland because of a well-founded fear of persecution. This diversity of ethnicity, education, and social class challenges us as pastors to welcome these new immigrants and help them join our communities in ways that are respectful of their cultures and in ways that mutually enrich the immigrants and the receiving Church.

To pursue this vision of unity in diversity, we have chosen the way marked out by Pope John Paul II as he stood beneath the figure of Our Lady of Guadalupe in Mexico City on January 22, 1999, and announced the summary of *Ecclesia in America*: namely, the call to conversion, communion, and solidarity.

The presence of so many people of so many different cultures and religions in so many different parts of the United States has challenged us as a Church to a profound conversion so that we can become truly a sacrament of unity. We reject the anti-immigrant stance that has become popular in different parts of our country, and the nativism, ethnocentricity, and racism that continue to reassert themselves in our communities. We are challenged to get beyond ethnic communities living side by side within our own parishes without any connection with each other. We are challenged to become an evangelizing Church open to interreligious dialogue and willing to proclaim the Gospel to those who wish to hear it. The new immigrants call most of us back to our ancestral heritage as descendants of immigrants and to our baptismal heritage as members of the body of Christ. "For in one Spirit we were all baptized into one body, whether Jews or Greeks, slaves or free persons, and we are all given to drink of one Spirit" (1 Cor 12:13).

The call to communion goes out to all members of the Church—bishops, priests, deacons, religious, lay leaders, and parishioners—to prepare themselves to receive the newcomers with a genuine spirit of welcome. Simple, grace-filled kindness and concern on the part of all parishioners to newcomers are the first steps. These can be accompanied by language and culture study as well

The presence of brothers and sisters from different cultures should be celebrated as a gift to the Church.

as constant and patient efforts at intercultural communication. The integration of incoming groups is complex because of multiple Mass schedules and lack of personnel or resources, but if the receiving parish staffs and parishioners are open to the newcomers and provide a bridge to join cultures to one another, the newcomers themselves will provide the leadership and show the way to a healthy integration. Both on parish and diocesan levels, the presence of brothers and sisters from different cultures should be celebrated as a gift to the Church through well-prepared liturgies, lay leadership development programs inclusive of all, the appointment of prepared leaders of immigrant communities to parish and diocesan positions, and special efforts to help youth find their way as they experience themselves often torn between two cultures.

One successful model of unity in diversity was Encuentro 2000: Many Faces in God's House, the National Conference of Catholic Bishops' celebration for the Jubilee Year. In the materials prior to the celebration, Encuentro 2000 offered a discussion method called the "mutual invitation process," which maximizes intercultural participation. In the celebration itself, Encuentro 2000 was an experience of the exuberance and vitality, the profound faith and devotional life of the participants. Encuentro 2000 also demonstrated that communion in a multicultural Church is a true possibility for the new millennium.

The call to solidarity can be summed up in Pope John Paul II's Message for World Migration Day 2000: "The Church hears the suffering cry of all who are uprooted from their own land, of families forcefully separated, of those who, in the rapid changes of our day, are unable to find a stable home anywhere. She senses the anguish of those without rights, without any security, at the mercy of every kind of exploitation, and she supports them in their unhappiness" (no. 6). We bishops commit ourselves and all the members of our church communities to continue the work of advocacy for laws that respect the human rights of immigrants and preserve the unity of the immigrant family. We encourage the extension of social services, citizenship classes, community organizing efforts that secure improved housing conditions, decent wages, better medical attention, and appropriate educational opportunities for immigrants and refugees. We advocate reform of the 1996 immigration laws that have undermined some basic human rights for immigrants. We join with others of good will in a call for legalization opportunities for the maximum number of undocumented persons, particularly those who have built equities and otherwise contributed to their communities.

In *Ecclesia in America,* Pope John Paul II calls for a "new evangelization" centered on the person of Jesus Christ. "'The encounter with the living Jesus Christ' is 'the path to conversion, communion and solidarity'" (no. 7). Such an encounter, so central to all our Jubilee Year activities, leads to a daily vision of the risen Lord, present and active in the world, especially in the poor, in the stranger, and in the migrant and refugee. These immigrants, new to our shores, call us out of our unawareness to a conversion of mind and heart through which we are able to offer a genuine and suitable welcome, to share together as brothers and sisters at the same table, and to work side by side to improve the quality of life for society's marginalized members. In so doing, we work to bring all the children of God into a fuller communion, "the communion willed by God, begun in time and destined for completion in the fullness of the Kingdom" (*Ecclesia in America,* no. 33).

INTRODUCTION:
AN IMMIGRANT CHURCH,
THEN AND NOW

"For I was hungry and you gave me food, I was thirsty and you gave me drink, a stranger and you welcomed me." (Mt 25:35)

On June 2, 2000, the Jubilee Day for Migrants and Refugees, Pope John Paul II looked out over a sunlit crowd of pilgrims gathered in St. Peter's Square from all nations: migrants, refugees, seafarers, Gypsies,[1] foreign students, circus and carnival workers, airport workers, truckers, all varieties of people on the move with their bishop promoters, their chaplains and spiritual directors. The pope celebrated the Eucharist, which drew that great diversity of people into unity in the communion of Father, Son, and Holy Spirit. He reminded them that in the Church they are meant to experience this trinitarian communion. In the Church their diversity is to be grounded in a profound unity. Through the members of the Church, solitary migrations are to end in the embrace of solidarity.

This jubilee vision of Pope John Paul II is the vision guiding us, the bishops of the United States, as we respond to the new immigrants who have recently come to our shores.

Encuentro 2000: Many Faces in God's House

As the celebration for the Jubilee Year 2000, the National Conference of Catholic Bishops sponsored Encuentro 2000. Throughout the jubilee year, thousands of people of many different cultures participated in discussion groups with a book entitled *Many Faces in God's House*. These parish groups used a discussion method called "mutual invitation process," which maximized the intercultural participation. These parish discussions and gatherings on diocesan and regional levels led to a national celebration in Los Angeles, July 6–9, 2000. All of these events honored and affirmed the many cultures in our Church. Encuentro 2000 was an opportunity for the Church in the United States to gather to engage in profound conversations about life and faith, to worship together, to forgive one another and be reconciled, to acknowledge unique histories, and to discover ways in which Catholic communities can be one Church from diverse cultures and ethnicities. More than 80 bishops and 5,000 representatives from 150 dioceses, all 50 states, and 157 different ethnic and cultural groups took part in the national event.

Twenty years ago in *Beyond the Melting Pot: Cultural Pluralism in the United States*, we the bishops of the United States noted that cultural pluralism was the common heritage of all Americans. As the new millennium unfolds, the "new immigration" from all the continents of the world calls attention to the reality of the United States as largely a "nation of immigrants" and to the diversity of national and ethnic origins of all people of this country. In this new context, the Catholic community is rapidly re-encountering itself as an "immigrant Church," a witness at once to the diversity of people who make up our world and to our unity in one humanity, destined to enjoy the fullness of God's blessings in Jesus Christ. This unity in diversity was celebrated at Encuentro 2000, sponsored as the National Conference of Catholic Bishops' principal jubilee celebration, highlighting "many faces in God's house."

A century ago, the Church responded generously to the needs of immigrants: building parishes and schools, establishing a vast array of charitable institutions, evangelizing newcomers, and being evangelized in turn by immigrant Catholics with distinctive traditions of worship and often a deep spirituality of their own. Members of the Eastern Catholic Churches arrived during the same period. They were not always understood by their fellow Catholics, although they were received and did develop as members of the Church in America. Despite the attacks of "nativists" and the criticisms made by English-speaking Catholics, national parishes were established that provided a safe haven where newcomers were able to pray and hear the word of God in their own languages, begin the education of their children in the language of the home, and so adapt to their new society with the security of community and faith. The Church embraced these immigrants, supporting them in their striving to build a better life and encouraging the efforts of many of them to help build a labor movement that could represent them in that struggle. And then, as now—despite the predictions of critics—immigrants and their children quickly became vital participants in

American society, acquiring proficiency in English by the second and third generations, rising in the educational system, and contributing in thousands of ways to the economic growth and social, political, and spiritual life of the country.

WHO ARE THE NEW IMMIGRANTS?

The "new" immigration to the United States stems from global changes—both economic and political—over the past forty years and from legal changes starting with the 1965 Immigration Act. The latter abolished the quota system that had systematically favored immigrants from Western Europe and had largely cut off immigration from Asia, Africa, and the Middle East after 1920. Meanwhile war, economic distress, the desire to be reunited with families, and the new legal opportunities since the 1960s have prompted a diverse immigration from Latin America and the Caribbean, Asia and the Pacific Islands, the Middle East, Africa, Eastern Europe, and the former Soviet Union and Yugoslavia.

While the new immigrants include many unskilled workers who perform difficult and menial tasks as in the past, the new immigrants also include many skilled workers, recruited to fill specialized positions as nurses, computer professionals, and scientists. The United States is thus the beneficiary of the years of education, training, and experience that come with these new workers. While we welcome all the new immigrants and recognize that our Church, like the United States as a whole, has come to depend upon the many talents and profound energy of newcomers, we must also remind our government that the emigration of talented and trained individuals from the poorer countries represents a profound loss to those countries. And we remind heads of government around the world that emigration of all kinds—but especially that of those fleeing war and persecution, famine and economic distress—is a sign of the failure of the whole international community to guarantee the security and welfare of all people in their homelands.

The ultimate resolution of the problems associated with forced migration and illegal immigration lies in changing the conditions that drive persons from their countries of origin. Accordingly, we urge the governments of the world, particularly our own government, to promote a just peace in those countries that are at war, to protect human rights in those countries that deny them, and to foster the economic development of those countries that are unable to provide for their own peoples. We also urge the governments of the "receiving" countries to welcome these immigrants, to provide for their immediate needs, and to enable them to come to self-sufficiency as quickly as possible.

THE MIGRATION FOR SURVIVAL

We must never forget that many immigrants come to this country in desperate circumstances. Some have fled political persecution, war, and economic devastation, particularly from Southeast Asia in the 1970s, Central America and the Caribbean in the 1980s, and the former Yugoslavia, the former Soviet Union, and

Africa in the 1990s. Others have wagered on finding a better life in this country in the face of economic desperation at home. As Pope John Paul II has noted, "In many regions of the world today people live in tragic situations of instability and uncertainty. It does not come as a surprise that in such contexts the poor and the destitute make plans to escape, to seek a new land that can offer them bread, dignity and peace. This is the migration of the desperate. . . . Unfortunately, the reality they find in host nations is frequently a source of further disappointment" (Message on World Migration Day 2000, no. 4).

Some refugees[2] have enjoyed the sanction and support of the U.S. government, while others have been denied attention and systematically deported, and some have been subjected to humiliating incarceration under deplorable conditions. Increasing numbers of refugees from the conflicts of the 1980s have seen their status adjusted to that of permanent residency; but disparities in treatment, complicated and drawn-out asylum procedures, and long waits for service contribute to the already difficult process of adjustment that individuals and families in flight have to face. Both individual lay people and church agencies have worked alongside secular organizations to correct these situations and address the sufferings of those caught up in the complex and bureaucratic U.S. immigration system whose policies often lead to the fragmenting of families, but more needs to be done.

Undocumented Immigrants
One reality remains constant in the American experience of immigration: the demand of the U.S. economy for unskilled labor—and the corresponding entrance of immigrants seeking work—in labor-intensive industries such as agriculture, construction, food processing, and services. Undocumented immigrants face special hardships in such areas. The Immigration and Naturalization Service estimates that three to four million undoc-

The Church supports the human rights of all people and offers them pastoral care, education, and social services, no matter what the circumstances of entry into this country.

umented workers hold jobs in this country, many of which are poorly paid, insecure, and dangerous. They face discrimination in the workplace and on the streets, the constant threat of arrest and deportation, and the fear that they or their children will be denied medical care, education, or job opportunities. Many have lived in the United States for years, establishing roots in their communities, building their families, paying taxes, and contributing to the economy. If arrested and deported, they leave behind children and sometimes spouses who are American citizens. While the changes in the law over the last several years have enabled many in this situation to adjust their status to that of permanent resident, the 1996 immigration legislation made this option more difficult for the vast majority. Without condoning undocumented migration, the Church supports the human rights of all people and offers them pastoral care, education, and social services, no matter what the circumstances of entry into this country, and it works for the respect of the human dignity of all—especially those who find themselves in desperate circumstances. We recognize that nations have the right to control their borders. We also recognize and strongly assert that all human persons, created as they are in the image of God, possess a fundamental dignity that gives rise to a more compelling claim to the conditions worthy of human life.

Accordingly, the Church also advocates legalization opportunities for the maximum number of undocumented persons, particularly those who have built equities and otherwise contributed to their communities.

IMMIGRANT FAMILIES AND THEIR COMMUNITIES

The vast majority of the 600,000 to 900,000 immigrants admitted annually to this country enter as immediate relatives of U.S. citizens or legal permanent residents, a trend that coincides with the Church's teaching supporting family reunification. At the same time, the family preference system continues to experience considerable backlogs, prolonging the separation of families. The 1996 immigration laws have torn apart families that have established themselves in the United States over many years, sometimes on the basis of minor criminal offences duly punished years ago.

Over a third of the new immigrants have become naturalized citizens, and the longer immigrants remain here the more likely they will become citizens; but here, too, the Church views with grave concern recent legislation[3] that has withdrawn basic benefits from legal residents who are not yet citizens and threatened the ability of many hard-working immigrants to remain in this country.

Immigrants experience the tensions of their new situation much more than the society around them does. They have settled in a foreign land with laws, customs, and a language that they must master sooner or later, often at great personal cost. They struggle to build community among themselves in hopes of providing the sense of continuity and security they need in order to face the new world they have chosen or were forced to accept. They do not want to give up all that they value in their own ways of life—nor do they want their children to grow up without those traditions. Thus, many households carry on, to one degree or another, the cultures of immigrant parents, and today, one in five Americans enjoys immediate ties to a heritage beyond our borders.

Ministry in Many Languages

Today many dioceses, from Miami to Amarillo, Texas, serve a majority Hispanic population. In Los Angeles, the growth in the archdiocese over the last two decades has mirrored perfectly the growth in the immigrant—especially Hispanic—population. Mass is said in more than fifty different languages in the Los Angeles archdiocese, where some fifty-five national groups are served by priests from their own countries of origin. The Diocese of Honolulu has long served a diverse community drawn from the islands of the Pacific and from Asia. Under its vicariate for ethnic ministries, the diocese has ministries to Chinese, Filipino, Hispanic, Japanese, Korean, Samoan, Tongan, and Vietnamese Catholics. The Archdiocese of Boston serves nine different African national groups, as well as ten Asian groups, Brazilians, Haitians, Hispanics from various parts of Latin America and the Caribbean, and immigrants from Europe. And the Diocese of Memphis has established ministries for Vietnamese, Polish, Native American, Filipino, and Korean Catholics, alongside older African American and Hispanic ministries. The Diocese of Stamford for Ukrainian Catholics has an office to minister to those who come from the former Soviet Union. These are just a few examples.

These realities ensure that few Americans have not encountered recent immigrants to this country in their neighborhoods and workplaces. Long Beach, California, is home to more Cambodians than Phnom Phen. Los Angeles ranks just behind Mexico City and Guadalajara in the number of residents of Mexican origin. Chicago at times has had more persons of Polish extraction than Warsaw. At the same time, rural towns and small cities throughout the country have begun to feel a presence of immigrants in their communities not seen since the great wave of immigration at the end of the nineteenth century.

*Immigrant communities provide
a growing percentage of the
vocations to the priesthood
and religious life as well as
lay leadership at the
service of the Church in
the United States.*

THE NEW IMMIGRATION AND THE CHURCH

Many of the new immigrants are Catholics. Probably more than
80 percent of Hispanic immigrants were raised in the Catholic
faith. By some estimates, Hispanic Catholics—including the
United States' large Puerto Rican and Mexican American populations[4]—could make up the majority of U.S. Catholics within the
next twenty years. But other immigrant populations also include
large numbers of Catholics. Filipinos, who represent almost 5 percent of the immigrant population, are overwhelmingly Catholic.
Some 350,000 of the 1.4 million Vietnamese immigrants in this
country are Catholic. These Catholics are joined by thousands of
Eastern Catholics coming from the former Soviet Union, the
Middle East, and India. A smaller but still significant number of
the Chinese, Korean, Japanese, Laotian, Sri Lankan, Indonesian,
Tongan, Samoan, and Asian Indian immigrants are also Catholic.
Among the increasing numbers of immigrants from Africa, many
are Catholics, raised in the vibrant Catholic culture of the Church's
fastest growing region.

Throughout the country, the liturgy and church decor increasingly reflect the cultural gifts of the new immigrants, with their own images of Mary and the saints, their songs, and their distinctive celebrations taking their place alongside those of older generations of immigrants. And immigrant communities provide a growing percentage of the vocations to the priesthood and religious life as well as lay leadership at the service of the Church in the United States today. The profile provided regarding the new immigrants who are Catholic should not minimize the Church's overwhelming concern for all new arrivals, regardless of their religious tradition or lack of one.

THE CALLING OF
THE CHURCH

I n this context of opportunity and challenge that is the new
immigration, we bishops of the United States reaffirm the
commitment of the Church, in the words of Pope John Paul
II, to work "so that every person's dignity is respected, the immigrant is welcomed as a brother or sister, and all humanity forms
a united family which knows how to appreciate with discernment the different cultures which comprise it" (Message for
World Migration Day 2000, no. 5). We call upon all people of
good will, but Catholics especially, to welcome the newcomers in
their neighborhoods and schools, in their places of work and
worship, with heartfelt hospitality, openness, and eagerness both
to help and to learn from our brothers and sisters, of whatever
race, religion, ethnicity, or background.

A TRADITION OF WELCOME AND
PASTORAL CONCERN

This call is based on the rich heritage of Scripture and the
Church's teaching. The patriarchs themselves were nomads.
Settled by the hand of God in the time of Abraham, they soon
migrated to Egypt, where they suffered oppression and were
delivered once again by God's hand. From this experience comes
a deep appreciation for the plight of the migrant, underlined in
the words of Scripture: "You shall not oppress an alien; you well

know how it feels to be an alien, since you were once aliens yourselves in the land of Egypt" (Ex 23:9). "You shall treat the stranger who resides with you no differently than the natives born among you, have the same love for him as for yourself; for you too were once strangers in the land of Egypt" (Lv 19:33-34). The Torah made special provisions for immigrants with the reminder that "you too were once slaves in Egypt" (Dt 16:9-12): "At the end of every third year you shall bring out all the tithes of your produce for that year and deposit them in community stores, that the Levite who has no share in the heritage with you, and also the alien, the orphan and the widow who belong to your community, may come and eat their fill; so that the LORD, your God, may bless you in all that you undertake" (Dt 14:28-29).

Indeed, the experience of exile, oppression, and deliverance to the Promised Land is the central act of the drama of salvation for Judaism. In honor of God's deliverance of his people, Israel was enjoined to show justice towards all: "For the LORD, your God, is the God of gods, the LORD of lords, the great God, mighty and awesome, who has no favorites, accepts no bribes; who executes justice for the orphan and the widow, and befriends the alien, feeding and clothing him. So you too must befriend the alien, for you were once aliens yourselves in the land of Egypt" (Dt 10:17-19). Jesus echoes this tradition when he proclaims prophetically, "For I was hungry and you gave me food, I was thirsty and you gave me drink, a stranger and you welcomed me" (Mt 25:35).

The Church has remained faithful to this call to care for migrants of all kinds and has responded accordingly over the centuries. The apostolic constitution *Exsul Familia*, promulgated by Pope Pius XII in 1952, takes its name from its evocation of the "émigré Holy Family of Nazareth, fleeing into Egypt," to which the pope pointed as "the archetype of every refugee family." Pope Pius XII recalls a long tradition of papal solicitude for immigrants and refugees, noting the hospitality to strangers and refugees traditionally provided by the Holy See and recalling the words of the Fourth Lateran Council of 1215: "We find in most countries, cities and dioceses people of diverse languages who, though bound by one Faith, have varied rites and customs. Therefore we strictly enjoin that the Bishops of these cities or dioceses provide the proper men, who will celebrate the Liturgical Functions according to their rites and languages." The pope cites with pride, as one proof of the Church's constant solicitude in this respect, the provisions for the establishment of "national parishes" in the United States in the nineteenth century to accommodate the immigrants of that era.

Eastern Catholic Churches in the U.S.A.

Today, we find scattered throughout the United States vibrant communities of Eastern Catholic Churches, including the ancient churches of India (the Malabar and Malankara Churches) and Ethiopia (the Ge'ez); the Coptic, Maronite, Syrian, and Chaldean Churches of Egypt and the Middle East; the Armenian Church; and the many Churches of the Byzantine tradition. Each has distinctive disciplines, liturgies, and theologies reaching back many hundreds of years, but all are part of the universal Church, as the Second Vatican Council reminds us (*Lumen Gentium*, no. 23).

The Second Vatican Council likewise called on the national bishops' conferences to pay special attention to those who "are not adequately cared for by the ordinary pastoral ministry of the parochial clergy or are entirely deprived of it," including "the many migrants, exiles and refugees," and to devise solutions for them (*Christus Dominus*, no. 18), a call endorsed by Pope Paul VI in approving a revision of church norms regarding pastoral care for immigrants. His *Instruction on the Pastoral Care of People Who Migrate* affirmed that "migrating people carry with them their own mentality, their own language, their own culture, and their own religion. All of these things are parts of a certain spiritual heritage of opinions, traditions and culture which will perdure outside the homeland. Let it be prized highly everywhere" (no. 11).

These words should apply with special force to members of the numerous Eastern Catholic Churches, who preserve ancient traditions of worship and practice reaching back to the days of the apostles. In full communion with the Catholic Church, they are the bearers of the authentic teachings of the Church, each according to their own traditions. Because of political upheaval, war, and religious persecution, the twentieth century saw an unprecedented emigration—one that continues today—of Eastern Catholics who are a minority in their countries of origin and who must struggle to maintain their faith and their traditions in the United States in the context of the predominant Latin Church.

Pope John Paul II urges in his apostolic letter *Orientale Lumen* that a "conversion is . . . required of the Latin Church, that she may respect and fully appreciate the dignity of Eastern Christians, and accept gratefully the spiritual treasures of which the Eastern Catholic Churches are the bearers, to the benefit of the entire catholic Communion" (no. 21).

The immigrants among us thus bring a richness that we are bound to embrace, for their sake and for our own. As Pope Paul VI noted, in words recently recalled by Pope John Paul II, "The Church can regard no one as excluded from its motherly embrace, no one as outside the scope of its motherly care. It has no enemies except those who wish to make themselves such. Its catholicity is no idle boast. It was not for nothing that it received its mission to foster love, unity and peace among men" (*Ecclesiam Suam*, no. 94). The way to achieve this mission was presented on January 22, 1999,

"The Church can regard no one as excluded from its motherly embrace, no one as outside the scope of its motherly care."

when Pope John Paul II stood beneath the image of Our Lady of Guadalupe in Mexico City and delivered to the whole Church the post-synodal apostolic exhortation *Ecclesia in America—On the Encounter with the Living Jesus Christ: The Way to Conversion, Communion and Solidarity in America*. This is the way we will follow in this document.

A CALL TO CONVERSION

Though we celebrate the diversity within our communities, we bishops must also confess that today, as in the past, the treatment of the immigrant too often reflects failures of understanding and sinful patterns of chauvinism, prejudice, and discrimination that deny the unity of the human family, of which the one baptism is our enduring sign. Such patterns, in the words of Pope John Paul II, "show the urgent need for a transformation of structures and a change of mentality, which is what the Great Jubilee of the Year 2000 asks of Christians and every person of good will" (Message for World Migration Day 2000, no. 1). For Catholics especially, a recognition of failures in the face of the opportunities and challenges of the new immigration should serve as a call to a renewal of baptismal vows, through repentance and a sharing in the mercy of the one Lord who would gather all to himself in the unity of the children of God.

We bishops must confess, as well, that recent immigrants have not always encountered welcome in the Church. Today immigrants of all sorts too often face prejudice within the Church. At times their legitimate desire to worship in their own language, according to their own traditions, has not been satisfied. Some have been turned away by pastors or find their petition for a Mass in their own language and a share in parish facilities opposed by members of the parish community. For those who live far from concentrated populations of people who share their heritage, there is often no alternative but to struggle through the English Mass while the deepest expressions of their spirit cry out silently in another language. Where the Church has not been welcoming, many have turned to other sources of community and religious fulfillment, but at the expense of abandoning the riches of their Catholic faith and native traditions.

FORGETFUL OF OUR HERITAGE

Perhaps the greatest obstacle to welcoming the stranger is that many Americans have forgotten their immigrant past. "Nativism" assumes that there is just one image of a "real American" and that immigrants either cannot live up to it or willfully refuse to do so. Originally directed against Catholics of all sorts, today such nativism can be seen in a campaign against "multiculturalism" in all its forms, on the premise that reverence for distinctive traditions and histories undermines the unity of American society. Like the Catholic "Americanizers" of the nineteenth century, who opposed the establishment of national parishes, the critics of multiculturalism today want immigrants and other distinctive groups to shed their languages, customs, and identities as quickly as possible, to become Americans "just like the rest of us." But "the rest of us" are, in fact, a culturally plural society—Catholics, Protestants, Jews, and Muslims; believers and non-believers; Southerners and Northerners; Irish, Italian, and Mexican—proud of our heritages and proud to be Americans, all at once.

A kind of nativism appears in the Church itself when established members insist that there is just one way to worship, one set of familiar hymns, one small handful of familiar devotions, one way to organize a parish community, one language for all—and that immigrants must adapt to that way of doing things. In doing so, such nativists forget not only that their ancestors spoke different languages and worshiped in different ways not long ago, but that their devotions and familiar saints, even their

Opening Doors to Many Cultures:
Nativity Parish in Washington, D.C.

In the first fifty years of its history, the Church of the Nativity of Our Lord Jesus in Washington, D.C., had a stable Caucasian community growing in the early 1950s to 15,000 members. When Archbishop Patrick O'Boyle integrated schools and parishes, the parish changed to mostly African American in almost ten years.

This was just the beginning of Nativity's multicultural experience. In the next years, the African American Catholic community welcomed neighbors from the Caribbean, Afro-Latinos, and Africans. In 1994, Nativity Parish opened its doors to the 400-family Nigerian Catholic community. At first, the communities went separate ways with resultant tensions. A breakthrough came on Holy Family Sunday when the first shared worship service was held. Many joyful shared services followed, especially with the visit of Nigerian bishops. Soon Nigerian children enrolled in school and in altar service. Nigerian adults joined finance and parish council positions and choirs. Nativity's members also include 150 Filipino families. The twelve-voice El Shaddai Choir joins at times with the Nigerian choir and the Gospel Choir for a joyous blend of voices and rhythms on special occasions. A common repertoire of congregational song is emerging.

As a result of the wars in Central America, more than 1,000 Latinos have moved into the parish. This influx has strained an already complex social situation, but the parish is working on ways to help the Hispanics by offering English classes, immigration assistance, and a youth and family center. The Archdiocese has funded a program to help make the Catholic School more accessible to Hispanics. The school now has an English as a Second Language counselor as well as Spanish in all eight grades. Add to that a small but growing French-speaking community from Haiti and other Francophone countries in the Caribbean and Africa. They have formed a French-speaking Renew 2000 group. Nativity is looking to continued growth as a parish family that models inclusion, hospitality, and evangelization.

patterns of church organization, sprang from encounters between differing traditions within the Church.

COMPETITION FOR RESOURCES

Competition for resources and recognition among the ethnic groups of the parish often centers on specifics such as Mass times, the use of facilities, and the attention of priests; but such conflicts can reflect vague fears that one group will somehow displace a long-established one. Established parishioners, used to thinking of their parish practices and religious traditions as the norm, may cling to their control over the parish council or "prime" Sunday Mass times. They may find themselves increasingly a minority and may react with fear to protect the parish where they were raised and where they saw their children baptized and educated in the faith. African American Catholics, who have their own history of having been excluded and discriminated against in the larger Church, as in society in general, now face newcomers in many of their parishes, newcomers who threaten their hold on the few institutions where they have come to feel at home. In some cases, multiple immigrant groups compete with one another within a single parish. In other cases, immigrant clergy struggle with their bishop or pastor for control over the finances of an immigrant group or for final authority over the congregation. While such competition can be destructive of community life, the issues involved are often real, and they require wisdom, much charity, and careful mediation to reach solutions that respect the legitimate concerns of all sides.

CULTURAL FEARS

The fears associated with encounters between groups are often difficult to overcome precisely because they are unacknowledged or unclear. Some are afraid because they do not know how to behave with others of a different culture. Others—in ignorance, relying on stereotypes—are convinced that those who are different are also

No culture is either permanent or perfect. All constantly need to be evangelized and uplifted by the good news of Jesus Christ.

somehow inferior: less educated, "dirty," or dangerous. Negative images and derogatory jokes and remarks readily merge with racism, America's "original sin," reinforcing the fear of the unknown in many people's minds by creating stereotypes about people whose facial features or skin color identify them as Asian, Arab, African, or Mexican. In some instances, racism has been so deeply ingrained that an institutional racism prevails. Racist attitudes can linger in subtle ways, even when people get to know one another in parish activities, unless we vigorously educate ourselves about our neighbors, learn to appreciate their heritages, encounter their own images of us, and strive to work with them on behalf of common causes.

Some of our fears are tied to what we see as defense of our own culture or way of life. Many people cling—rightfully so—to their distinctive culture. They fear the loss of their own familiar ways of doing things as they encounter new images and practices of community life and worship that are foreign to them. Immigrants themselves often fear other groups and worry that their children will lose the values of the homeland, come to show disrespect towards their parents and elders, and exchange their own culture for the consumer values of the surrounding society. Such concerns are well founded, and they compound the difficulties of adaptation to a new setting as both host and immigrant react, each against the other, in fear of change.

Change, however, is inevitable as immigrants set down roots in this country, enriching American culture while adopting aspects of it themselves. Indeed, it would be a mistake to regard any culture as fixed and immutable. All cultures are in constant processes of change as their members seek new ways to address individual and group needs and as they encounter new situations and other cultures. Indeed, no culture is either permanent or perfect. All constantly need to be evangelized and uplifted by the good news of Jesus Christ. The encounter between cultures that is an everyday affair in the incorporation of immigrants into the Church and the communities of the United States should provoke not only adaptation on both sides but a critical discernment of the strengths and failings of each culture in the light of the Gospel.

INSTITUTIONAL OBSTACLES

Institutional inadequacies have also impeded the full-fledged welcome and communion to which the Church is called. Parish and diocesan structures have not always been flexible enough to accommodate sudden influxes of new groups. Parishes have found themselves serving faith communities that draw members from far outside parish boundaries, raising questions about the sources and limits of parish resources. And regrettably, some parishes have found that their parishioners have imbibed the post-1960s societal attitude of exclusion of new immigrants. In many cases, immigrant Catholics have been attracted to evangelical and Pentecostal churches, leaving behind their Catholic faith.

Many pastors struggle to accommodate separate worship communities who celebrate their faith in their native tongues within the same parish. Pastors strive to meet the needs of multiple culturally diverse groups who are too small to support their own eucharist and specialized programs. Similarly, pastors who wish to serve whoever approaches the altar may lack the experience or the models to know how to reach out to newcomers who are not Catholic or whose Catholicism has not included a regular liturgical life or whose faith is tied more closely to home and family than to the parish community.

Immigrant communities must find priests willing and able to minister in their language and a place to gather for worship and community activities. They are often at a loss as to how to supply themselves with liturgical texts and educational materials and how to develop a sense of communion with a diocese whose language is not their own. They struggle to balance the competing demands of U.S. schools and the larger culture on their youth with their own desires to benefit their children with traditional values and culture. Immigrant priests may find themselves jealous of their own autonomy and better able to relate to their own priests' associations and dioceses of origin than to the priests and diocese of their U.S. home, where they may feel a lack of welcome.

The tensions and debates occasioned by such concerns can sometimes lead to greater understanding within the Church. But they can also lead, in the extreme, to painful schisms and the alienation of the faithful from the Church. Taken together—and despite the efforts of many dioceses—such tensions make clear that the Church has not adequately addressed the host of questions that

The Church of the twenty-first century requires a profound conversion in spirit and in its institutions to reflect its own cultural pluralism.

surround pastoral ministry to the new immigrants. In this and the other respects mentioned above, the Church of the twenty-first century requires a profound conversion in spirit and in its institutions to reflect its own cultural pluralism, to address the needs of the whole Catholic community, and to further a genuine communion and solidarity among the diverse members of the Body of Christ.

This debate on the effective and adequate response of current church institutions to the new immigrant reality echoes the discussion in the Synod of America and *Ecclesia in America* on the effectiveness of parish structures:

> Because of the particular problems they present, special attention needs to be given to parishes in large urban areas, where the difficulties are such that normal parish structures are inadequate and the opportunities for the apostolate are significantly reduced. The institution of the parish, however, retains its importance and needs to be preserved. For this, there is a need "to keep looking for ways in which the parish and its pastoral structures can be more effective in urban areas." (no. 41)

A CALL TO COMMUNION

As Catholics we are called to take concrete measures to overcome the misunderstanding, ignorance, competition, and fear that stand in the way of genuinely welcoming the stranger in our midst and enjoying the communion that is our destiny as Children of God. We commit ourselves, accordingly, to working to strengthen understanding among the many cultures that share in our Catholic faith, to promoting intercultural communication among our people, and to seeing that those in ministry to our communities gain the language and cultural skills necessary to minister to the immigrants in our midst.

COMING TO UNDERSTAND OTHERS AS THE FIRST FORM OF HOSPITALITY

Time and time again, Pope John Paul II has echoed the teachings of his predecessors and of the Second Vatican Council that "it is one of the properties of the human person that he can achieve true and full humanity only by means of culture" (*Gaudium et Spes*, no. 53) and that to take away a person's culture is therefore to damage human dignity grievously. Communion does not abolish differences but brings together one family, diverse and united in the one Lord. Pope Paul VI urged that "it must be avoided that these diversities and adaptations in accordance with the various ethnical groups, even though legitimate, result in harm to that unity to which all are called in the Church" (*Pastoralis Migratorum Cura*). Thus, the Church's norms for the pastoral care of immigrants attempt to balance the legitimate rights of immigrants with their duty to look to

Bringing Gifts and Sharing Cultural Riches: *Simbang Gabi*

Simbang Gabi—literally, "going to church in the evening"—is the traditional pre-Christmas novena of the Philippines. This nine-day novena of Masses, usually starting on the evening of December 16, takes place in the parish church. Catechesis on gospel values in the Filipino culture, on Mary, and on her role in the Incarnation are strong points of *Simbang Gabi.*

Simbang Gabi manifests the Filipino rite of celebrating life in more festive ways through prayers, music, Christmas images, and symbols integrated in the nine days of liturgical celebrations. And as is customary in Filipino gatherings, after the Mass and catechesis, celebration continues with a variety of native dinners shared by the worshiping community.

The Filipino immigrants have introduced *Simbang Gabi* in their local parishes in the United States. In Chicago, where as many as fifty parishes have a significant Filipino presence, the celebration is widespread. Teresita Nuval, the Asian/Pacific Ministries Diocesan Director, explains that *Simbang Gabi* has been taken up by many U.S. pastors, even in parishes where there are few Filipinos, because they see the significance of celebrating Christmas as a faith experience as a healthy antidote to the prevailing materialism of current practice. In Los Angeles, *Simbang Gabi* has become an interparochial and multiethnic celebration. In Houston, Miami, Seattle, and other cities throughout the country, it is gaining acceptance, alongside the more familiar *Posadas*, as a way of enriching the celebration of Christmas for Catholics of all cultural backgrounds. In Honolulu, the Masses are celebrated at dawn (*Missa Aguinaldo/Missa de Gallo*), followed by a community breakfast.

the common good of both their communities of origin and their host community (*Instruction on the Pastoral Care of People Who Migrate*, nos. 5-11).

The Church embraces the rich cultural pluralism of this immigrant nation—what some call its "multicultural" reality.[5] Pope John Paul II insists that "the immigrant members of the Church, while freely exercising their rights and duties and being in full

ecclesial communion in the particular churches, feeling themselves Christians and brothers towards all, must be able to
remain completely themselves as far as language, culture, liturgy
and spirituality, and particular traditions are concerned"
(Address for World Migrants' Day, July 16, 1985). Indeed, the
pope warns repeatedly against attempting to rush a process of
assimilation or cultural adaptation in the name of unity, because
the goal is the mutual enrichment of peoples, not their assimilation to one way of being human. Thus the pope reached out to
refugees in the camp at Phanat Nikon, Thailand, in November
1984, saying, "My heart is with you. Have faith in yourselves.
Don't forget your identity as a free people with your own legitimate place in this world. Don't lose your distinctive personality
as a people! Remain firmly rooted in your respective cultures.
The world needs to learn more from you and to join in appreciation of your uniqueness."

The pope teaches that immigrants must guard their cultures for the
enrichment of the world. But the cultures of immigrants will only
be able to enrich this country when all Americans—recent immigrants and those long settled in this country—open their hearts and
minds to their neighbors and come to appreciate the diverse cultures that make up this society. Knowledge of cultures cannot just
come from books, but must come from the concrete efforts of individuals to get to know their neighbors, in all their diversity.

The welcome and hospitality that we ask our parishes to extend to
newcomers must include active efforts on the part of the pastor
and parish staff, individuals and families, parish councils, liturgy
committees, social concern entities, youth groups, and other parish
organizations to undertake the special effort necessary to learn
about the cultures in their midst and to exchange visits with worship communities and parishes where different cultural groups
make their homes. Special events such as international dinners,

common social events, and multicultural parish feasts can help to introduce the various members of the parish to other cultures and can lead to greater exchanges between groups. The parish is encouraged to sponsor forums in which members of different cultures can openly share their unique backgrounds and identify areas of unity.

The eucharistic celebration is central to church life and to our communion as Catholics with one another in the one Lord. Whenever the diverse cultures of parish and diocese are able to share the Eucharist in special celebrations that reflect the cultural riches of the participants, the Church demonstrates in the sacrament of our unity the multicultural face of the Church, proclaiming "with joy and firm faith that God is communion, Father, Son and Holy Spirit, unity in distinction, and that he calls all people to share in that same Trinitarian communion" (*Ecclesia in America*, no. 34).

INTERCULTURAL COMMUNICATION

Efforts to learn and worship together may come to nothing at all—or even reinforce prejudices—unless they are carried out with a spirit of openness and charity. Not everything in one culture will meet with the approval of another. There may be disagreements about child-rearing practices, the place of women in the liturgy, styles of preaching, or suitable expressions of piety. Such differences are inevitable even within one culture. But in cross-cultural encounters, disagreements must be informed by understanding the roots of people's attitudes and practices and with respect for their right to find their own way within the one Gospel. Understanding will come with a growing knowledge of the history, values, and experiences of others. Respect must be born of charity and faith in the ultimate unity in Christ of all humanity.

Intercultural communication—sustained efforts, carried out by people of diverse cultures, to appreciate their differences, work

Gathering Those Who are Scattered Abroad: Ministering to the Kmhmu' in California

Fr. Don MacKinnon had worked for years in one of San Francisco's toughest neighborhoods when he was asked to help a small group of refugees from the mountains of Laos. He found people who were desperately poor, with little knowledge of how to manage in the unfamiliar surroundings of northern California's populous East Bay communities, but eager for ministry in their own language. He was joined by Sr. Michaela O'Connor in this new apostolate.

The Kmhmu' language has no formal script or written tradition. Fr. MacKinnon and Sr. Michaela had to set out to learn the language the child's way: by immersion in the life of the community. At the same time, they were determined to provide the liturgy for this scattered group in the Kmhmu' language. They began by recording hymns. The community eagerly circulated the tapes among their members throughout northern California and to a distant community in New York. When they had sufficient command of the language, they videotaped the Mass in Kmhmu'. Then they turned to the problem of developing a script and began recording the community's songs and prayers in their language.

Most of Fr. MacKinnon's and Sr. Michaela's time is taken up with the day-to-day effort to help people with the legal and economic problems of settling in a new world. Their efforts to provide the liturgy in the Kmhmu' language, nevertheless, give the Kmhmu' a sense of pride and belonging that enables them to face the daily struggle.

out conflicts, and build on commonalities—will thus be an important component of coming to know and respect the diverse cultures that make up today's Church. The dominant culture in the United States stresses the individual and his or her feelings and decisions. In less individualistic cultures, individuals may feel hesitant to express their own opinions openly, even in a friendly setting, without reinforcement from the group. Among immigrants of the same group, too, divisions along lines of social class or educational background can erect barriers to understanding, with some members adapting to the procedures and practices of parish life more readily than others. Often, culturally sensitive intermediaries are needed to facilitate exchanges, mediate conflicts, and promote genuine participation by all.

Integration will be facilitated when all parties maintain an open spirit. Integration cannot be forced, and those who host newcomers must be especially aware of the vulnerabilities of immigrants and the impulse many immigrants feel to withdraw from interaction. Pastors and lay leaders who are aware of these dynamics of adaptation and communication among cultures will lead the way in facilitating the full, equal incorporation of all members of the community into the life of the Church.

LANGUAGES FOR MINISTRY

Special efforts to acquire the languages of the new immigrants by all church ministers constitute an essential, concrete step towards a full and effective welcome. In some cases, immigrant groups have brought with them significant numbers of priests and religious. This is true of the Vietnamese community, which has continued to produce vocations in large numbers in this country. In other cases, the home country's Church is sufficiently strong to send priests and religious to the United States to minister to immigrant communities from that country, as was the case in earlier waves of migration to this country. In many cases today, however, there are many immigrants but few priests, and dioceses must make special provisions to find or train priests, religious, and lay people capable of ministering to the newcomers in their own languages and cultures. Missionary orders have contributed magnificently to filling this need. In some dioceses, every seminarian is required to master a language other than English relevant to ministry to local immigrant communities. This practice should be encouraged throughout the United States. Priests, seminarians, religious, and lay ministers should all be encouraged to learn a language and acquire cultural knowledge relevant to their ministry.[6] Study abroad is generally the best way to do this, and it should be widely encouraged.

Especially in the case of some of the smaller immigrant groups, priests may have only a rudimentary knowledge of the language of the group they serve. Then they must depend upon religious, lay leaders, deacons, and trained catechists to ensure an effective ministry. And even where priests with the necessary language skills are available, it is important that other members of the larger community acquire the ability to communicate with immigrants in their own languages as part of a wider effort to develop more inclusive relations at the parish and diocesan levels, carry on the necessary work of evangelization, and promote diocesan programs capable of genuinely uniting diverse communities. The clergy and lay leaders should acquire a proficiency in English as quickly as possible and continue to improve their public speaking skills in English so as to further the communion of their communities with the wider Church in the United States. Parishes should provide opportunities for immigrants, including the elderly, to acquire proficiency in the English language.

Ministry in a Multicultural Church

Language acquisition on behalf of intercultural communication and effective ministry is just one practical step towards the fuller incorporation of the new immigrants into our communities. The Church as an institution needs to undertake other practical steps at national, diocesan, and parish levels.

Celebrating the Many Cultures of the Diocese: Oakland's Chautauqua Festival

Every year since 1992, the Diocese of Oakland holds its Chautauqua celebration of unity in the diversity of the Church. ("Chautauqua" is a Native American word meaning "gathering of peoples.") Chautauqua in the Oakland diocese begins with a procession and eucharistic liturgy led by the bishop, featuring choirs from a number of the ethnic groups that make up the diocese. The eucharistic celebration is followed by cultural entertainment, dancing, music, and ethnic foods. As Sr. Felicia Sarati of Oakland's Ethnic Pastoral Centers puts it, "Throughout the year, it's Poles with Poles, Koreans with Koreans. With Chautauqua we all come together." Besides the annual Chautauqua event, leaders of the diverse ethnic communities meet once a month to discuss concerns and welcome newcomers.

Oakland's Catholic community is indeed diverse. Besides older immigrant communities such as African Americans, Portuguese, Filipinos, and the numerous Catholics of Mexican descent, there are Asian Indians, Chinese, Vietnamese, Brazilians, Indonesians, Koreans, Poles, Catholics from the South Sea kingdom of Tonga, Eritreans (Ge'ez), Haitians, and even a small tribal group from Laos called Kmhmu'. What brings all these groups together is the spirit of welcome in the diocese and continuing attempts to provide for their spiritual needs.

National or Regional Level

At the national or regional level, efforts must be made to provide liturgical and catechetical materials for communities who do not have ready access to such materials in their language. Most dioceses lack the resources to provide such materials for more than one or two groups. Similarly, diocesan seminaries and lay ministry training programs are often ill-equipped to provide priests, religious, and lay leaders with the full range of linguistic, cultural, and intercultural communication training necessary to serve even local needs.

Efforts to redress these problems could be furthered by the creation of regional pastoral centers, serving the needs of one or several immigrant ethnic communities and financed by the dioceses they serve. Such centers could encourage theological reflection based on the traditions and experience of the various national churches represented in our immigrant communities. They could provide the translation services mentioned above and serve as a source for liturgical and catechetical materials for the communities they represent, as well as develop training materials for pastors, religious, and lay leaders in these communities. And they could offer training for all those involved in ministry to specific groups within the dioceses of their regions, extending the range of possibilities of language education, intercultural communication training, and education for ministry in a multicultural Church more generally.

Diocesan Level

Dioceses are the best equipped to address the multiple needs of the contemporary Church at the local level. The bishop as pastor of a diverse people has the care for all that concerns their life together. Thus, in developing diocesan policies and programs responsive to the reality of today's immigrant Church, bishops must take care to both respect the dignity of the diverse communities of the diocese

Personal Parishes and Missions: Meeting the Needs of Diverse Communities in Miami and New Orleans

The Diocese of Miami is home to 150,000 Haitian immigrants, most of them recently arrived. Many are poor, and though they are gradually learning English, the vibrant community life in Miami's "Little Haiti" is conducted mostly in the Creole language. In the early 1980s Fr. Thomas Wenski, now auxiliary bishop of Miami, convinced the diocese to establish a Haitian mission in a former Catholic girls' school. The diocese bore the costs of renovation, and the Notre Dame d'Haiti Mission was established.

With five Masses a week in Creole, the mission now serves 4,500 Haitians. The adjoining Haitian Catholic Center sees an average of 1,000 people a day for English classes, daycare, legal services, and catechism classes. Miami now has three Haitian missions in addition to numerous parishes that offer a Creole Mass or two. Some longer-established Haitians attend Mass in English at parishes throughout the city, but continued migration means that the missions will continue to provide essential outreach to the Haitian community.

The Diocese of New Orleans similarly welcomed a massive influx of Vietnamese refugees in the late 1970s. Led by Msgr. Dominic Luong, who left a teaching post in a New York seminary to champion the cause of his people, and with the help of Catholic Charities, the Vietnamese eventually settled in several parts of the city. The diocese established five missions to serve the community, centered on the Vietnamese Apostolate Center directed by Msgr. Luong. With the change in canon law in 1983, Msgr. Luong and his fellow Vietnamese priests established a personal parish at the center, now Mary Queen of Vietnam National Parish, with four missions under its wing. Today, there are two personal parishes, each with its own missions.

and draw them to unity in the one Church, striking that balance between the legitimate rights of immigrants to worship according to their own traditions and the concern for the common life of the Church in the United States. Diocesan authorities must decide when and how to honor the desire of immigrant groups for their own chapel, mission, or personal parish; how to foster a spirit of openness and welcome towards immigrant communities within parishes; how to promote the effective evangelization of all members of the local church and of those outside the Church; and how to bring together peoples of all the diverse cultures of the Church into one community.

We bishops commit ourselves with renewed energy to display a spirit of welcome, and we encourage all those involved in ministry to share in that spirit. We will look to the successful models of the past, such as the national parish, or contemporary practices in other dioceses, and adapt them to the needs and circumstances of our own dioceses. In each of our dioceses we will build up programs of ministry to immigrants and support them with new resources to the extent possible, in recognition of the growing contributions of our immigrant communities to the larger Church, and we will insist that pastors lend their support. Our diocesan seminaries must prepare seminarians for ministry to the Church of the twenty-first century. At the same time, we will devote resources to developing programs of cultural understanding and intercultural communication for religious and lay ministers. We bishops have a special responsibility to address questions of social justice for migrants of all sorts, participating in national and local efforts to combat discrimination and ensure equitable treatment under the law to all.

In the past, personal parishes were established successfully in some places to accommodate the needs and desires of strong, local immigrant communities. At the same time, not all groups have had the financial resources or numbers to sustain a parish of their own. Dioceses may need to develop guidelines to help parishes or deaneries respond to smaller or more dispersed groups so that they sense that they are welcome and have facilities appropriate to their needs.

Incorporating a Ministry of Welcome into Diocesan Structures: Memphis

The Diocese of Memphis saw a need for comprehensively incorporating into diocesan programs a ministry to the growing numbers of Catholics from all parts of the world. The chart shows how that diocese has organized its programs.

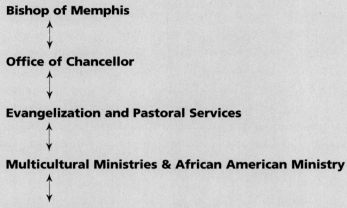

Bishop of Memphis

Office of Chancellor

Evangelization and Pastoral Services

Multicultural Ministries & African American Ministry

Ten Divisions

Council for African American Catholic Ministry
Hispanic Ministry
Vietnamese Ministry
Polish Catholic Mission
Native American Ministry
Filipino American Prayer Group
Korean Catholic Station
Multicultural Services & Programs/Workshops
Africentric Liturgies & Programs/Workshops
Multicultural Resources

Most dioceses have already provided modest resources to offices of ethnic ministry. The more these offices can be led by members of the communities being served, the better. In some cases, the bishop has appointed a vicar in charge of ministry to larger or more dispersed groups. In a few dioceses, Hispanic ministry in particular has been integrated into all of the offices of the diocese, providing constant feedback on how to address the needs of the Hispanic community within the various diocesan programs. In many dioceses, offices of ethnic ministry are able to ensure that parish positions are filled so as to serve the immigrant communities within the diocese. And many dioceses have designed diocesan-wide events to bring together the various cultures of the Catholic community. All of these efforts need to be studied and strengthened as the Church in the United States strives to celebrate the many gifts that immigrant communities bring to the Church in America.

Parish Level

Immigrants will experience the Church's welcome most personally at the level of the parish. Pastors and parish staff, accordingly, must be filled with a spirit of welcome, responding to a new and perhaps little-understood culture. They will be able to do so precisely to the extent that they have received the support of the diocese and the training that should go with it. A pastor with an open and welcoming spirit who insists that the whole parish participate in such a spirit can make a tremendous difference in relations among different groups. Pastors need to know about effective models for accommodating multiple cultural groups within a single parish structure. At the same time, the effort to mediate competing demands for facilities and lingering rivalries among groups requires sensitivity to the needs and styles of both cultures, as well as patience, charity, and communications skills. Pastors should make every effort to assist and encourage Eastern Catholics to find parishes that offer pastoral care according to their own traditions and rites. In the past immigrants belonging to Eastern Catholic churches were lost to those churches because of the lack of Eastern Catholic clergy, churches, and services. Sometimes they were joined to the Latin church, regrettably because of social and demographic pressures. Membership in a particular church of the immigrant (e.g., Eastern Catholic Church) must be respected.

Reaching out to immigrants who are not Catholics or who, though Catholic, have not yet participated fully in the life of the parish requires language and cultural skills, as well as an evangelical zeal that will need to be developed among more pastors, associates, religious, and lay people through outreach committees or census programs. Lay people, especially those who share language and cultural background with the immigrant group, can be invaluable bridges in efforts to incorporate immigrant communities into the life of the parish and reach out to non-believers among the new immigrants. In many of the countries from which the new immigrants come, it was the lay catechist who led people to conversion or a deeper appreciation of the faith. Lay catechists were the leaders and evangelizers of their people. Their ministry needs to be reaffirmed and strengthened in the new context.

Catholic Charities offers comprehensive services in most dioceses. Pastors can look to Catholic Charities for help in their response to new immigrants. Social service, legal assistance, and adult education programs—including English as a second language, parenting, job

44

Integrating a Multicultural Parish

Fr. Italo Dell'Oro was himself a young immigrant priest with no parish experience when he was made pastor of Assumption Parish in Houston. The parish had originally been the Italian parish of the diocese, but as Catholics of other backgrounds—Polish, Czech, German, and others—moved in, the parish attempted to accommodate them. When Fr. Dell'Oro arrived the parish council had no Hispanic representatives, although almost half the parish was Hispanic. The council used Robert's Rules of Order and resisted any attempts to discuss parish goals. In desperation Fr. Dell'Oro adopted the new diocesan guidelines for parish councils, including the optional discernment process to choose council members and guide the work of the body. An experienced facilitator from the chancery helped to organize the elections and guide the re-established council on their first retreat.

The result was a broadly representative council, with half the members being Hispanic and the others drawn from Italian, Irish, Polish, English, and German backgrounds. Better yet, the new councillors regard themselves as "a representative body, not a body of representatives" of competing factions. At parish council meetings, decisions are made by consensus.

A Hispanic committee continues to oversee the two Spanish-language Masses every Sunday, as well as activities for the Hispanic community. Fr. Dell'Oro has encouraged it to participate in fundraising for all-parish activities. One example: the renovation of the church, paid for through parish fund-raising activities, features a mural of the Assumption of Mary, with images of Pope John Paul II, Mother Seton, Archbishop Oscar Romero, and Juan Diego at her feet.

For many years, the Sunday procession at Pentecost has featured each of the older ethnic groups giving readings in their own languages. Now those languages include Spanish, and there are bilingual celebrations on Holy Thursday, the Easter Vigil, and the Vigil of the Assumption, as well.

Reaching Out Through Social Services: St. Thomas Aquinas Parish's Asian Center in South Philadelphia

When Fr. Arthur Taraborelli was growing up, St. Thomas Aquinas Parish served a solidly Italian neighborhood. Today, he is pastor of his old church, and the parish, though still predominantly Italian, is changing with the influx of refugees from Southeast Asia. Initially, the newcomers were met with suspicion and some fear, but Fr. Taraborelli and his assistant, Vietnamese-born Fr. Joseph Dinh Huynh, insisted that the parish had to open its arms to its new neighbors. A Vietnamese-language Mass was scheduled, and Vietnamese prayers and the new Vietnamese choir could be heard at special parish celebrations.

In 1988, the parish founded the Asian Social Service Center in part of the parish school building to provide immigration services and English language classes to recent immigrants, including Vietnamese, Chinese, Cambodians, Laotians, and Filipinos. Fr. Huynh had gotten to know each of the 611 Asian families in the parish, Catholic and non-Catholic alike, and found that language classes were a pressing need. Today, some 1,300 families of Asian ancestry come to the parish for classes and religious and cultural events, including Vietnamese New Year, which is celebrated with both a Mass and traditional Vietnamese rituals. Though most of those who attend are of other faiths, increasing numbers appear at the regular Sunday Mass, and the parish has seen nearly one hundred conversions.

training programs, and citizenship classes—can serve as valuable outreach to newcomers. The parish can also provide immigrants with forums for addressing social, emotional, and economic needs. Models and methods of a genuinely evangelical parish life need to be developed and disseminated so that pastors and lay leaders may choose among those best adapted to providing effective outreach to newcomers. In some cases, individual pastors or consortia of parishes, sometimes in conjunction with congregations of other faiths or secular organizations, can create immigration and social service agencies to serve particular neighborhoods.

At the same time, parishes can become sites for dialogue and cooperation, not only with the Protestant denominations that share our common Christian faith, but also with Buddhists, Hindus, Muslims, Jews, and others. Despite differences, all share common goals of providing for the religious and material needs of immigrant communities, and all have much to gain by working together.

Today's immigrants bring a vast richness of gifts, from new spiritual movements to a renewal of devotion to Mary in the great variety of national devotions, such as that to Our Lady of Guadalupe. In many dioceses, a renewal of vocations to the priesthood and religious life is one evident fruit of the new immigration, while lay participation in ministry has blossomed in many ethnic ministries.

The Special Needs of Youth

Of special concern are the youth of immigrant communities. Some are themselves immigrants, who despite a facility for acquiring English may feel especially torn between their original culture and that of their new home—fully at home in neither one culture nor the other. Others were born in this country, and though their first language may have been that of their parents, they quickly acquire the fluency of a native not only in the English language but in the prevailing culture in their schools and neighborhoods. In either case, young people may find themselves frequently in conflict with their parents and

Generations Joined by Faith

Each year the Hmong community gathers all its members for an annual retreat. Teenagers accompany adults in a weekend of formation and celebration. The teenagers are led in separate sessions by Fr. Joe Hirsch of the Diocese of LaCrosse, Wisconsin, who has learned enough of the Hmong language to read the ordinary prayers of the Mass and to teach Hmong songs and hymns. The teenagers' formation sessions are in English, their discussions in the Hmong language, and their liturgies in both languages, while their parents conduct their sessions only in the Hmong language.

Teenagers join their parents for morning and evening prayers. At the closing celebration, the Hmong teenagers entertain their parents and grandparents with both traditional Hmong dances and modern break-dances. The interaction bridges the generations and the cultures, preserving Hmong traditions, passing on the faith, and giving parents and teenagers alike a way to incorporate both Hmong and American cultures into their common life.

elders over ways of behaving and speaking, values, and beliefs, as they become "American" while living within an immigrant household and community that retain the country of origin's culture. Such conflicts are painful for both sides, and one or the other may call upon the Church to defend its particular claims and values. Young people can also experience conflict with peers who—because of insecurity or insensitivity—cause unnecessary division.

The Church recognizes the centrality of the family in the upbringing of the young and cherishes the great value that many immigrant cultures place upon the family. At the same time, it also has a duty to provide for the young as they struggle for their own identity and their own adaptation within the larger culture. Recreational, educational, and spiritual programs for youth can provide opportunities for helping them to understand and accommodate the claims of their parents while accepting what is wholesome in the culture around them. These programs can also help young people live in harmony with their peers. Everyday pastoral care and special programs for parents can help them understand and accept the struggles of their children, even as they reinforce the confidence that their children have already assimilated much of what they have to teach them despite the dissensions of the moment. Religious education programs can play a special role here in attempting to bridge the gap between cultures within the context of the one faith and to help the young deal positively with the tensions and difficulties they face.

In some instances, families are drawn to the parish precisely to take advantage of the school. Their immersion in their children's education puts them into regular contact with parish personnel and members of other cultural groups. In other cases, immigrants have had no experience of Catholic schools in their country of origin and require the encouragement (and often financial aid) of the parish to take advantage of this opportunity. Catholic schools can provide the children of immigrants with opportunities to adapt to American culture in a context permeated by the faith and in an atmosphere of hospitality to all cultures, and they can do much to promote cultural understanding and respect among parents and students alike. Catholic schools can also be powerful instruments of evangelization for immigrant communities who, though outside the Church, find in the schools a welcoming and supportive environment for the education of their children. But for a great many immigrants, none of this can be accomplished unless Catholic schools are made affordable for the poorer members of the community, a goal to which the diocese may have to contribute through sister-parish arrangements or outright grants of diocesan funds.

THE CALL TO SOLIDARITY

The Gospel calls us to solidarity with those who are suffering, vulnerable, and in need. In this spirit we recall the words of Pope John Paul II, who proclaimed, "The Church hears the suffering cry of all who are uprooted from their own land, of families forcefully separated, of those who, in the rapid changes of our day, are unable to find a stable home anywhere. She senses the anguish of those without rights, without any security, at the mercy of every kind of exploitation, and she supports them in their unhappiness" (Message for World Migration Day 2000, no. 6). Among today's immigrants, those who have fled war, famine, civil unrest, and economic desperation deserve our special understanding and support; but seafarers, those in the aviation world, and migrant workers, too, suffer uprootedness, discrimination, and injustice, along with all people on the move: circus and carnival workers, truckers, tourists, pilgrims, Gypsies, and Irish travelers.

In an age of economic globalization, a special concern of a culture of solidarity must be the migrant worker, both rural and urban. These laborers are vital to our agricultural, construction, service, and tourist industries. From the time they leave their homes to the time they arrive at their place of work, these migrant workers—forced to search for a basic livelihood for their families—face hazardous border crossings. (In the past five years, more than 500 have died at the U.S.–Mexico border because of increased border enforcement.) They are vulnerable

The Gospel Does Not Discriminate

For Fr. Kenneth DeGroot, O.Pream., the decision to invite the local Hispanic community to become a part of St. Willebrord's Parish, in Green Bay, Wisconsin, had nothing to do with legal status: "We never ask if they are 'legal' or 'illegal,' if they are documented or undocumented. We really believe that those who come to us have spiritual and physical needs, and we try to do what we can to serve them. We treat them as people who come to us in need, and we give them whatever services we are able. And I believe that is the mission of the Church."

to exploitation and abuse in transit, in border regions, and in the workplace. We bishops pledge ourselves, in the spirit of *Ecclesia in America,* to work in solidarity with the bishops of the migrants' countries of origin to provide for the safety, the basic needs, the human rights, and the effective pastoral care of these migrant workers. One of the propositions of the Synod of America asserts, "The Church in America must be a vigilant advocate, defending against any unjust restriction the natural right of individual persons to move freely within their own nation and from one nation to another. Attention must be called to the rights of migrants and their families and to respect for their human dignity, even in cases of non-legal immigration" (*Ecclesia in America,* no. 65).

Solidarity with migrants and refugees will take many forms, from participating in efforts to ensure that the U.S. government respect the basic human rights of all immigrants, to providing direct assistance to immigrants through diocesan and parish programs. Particularly vulnerable are the immigrant elderly who often find themselves isolated in their new country, lacking in language skills and in the family and community support system that they enjoyed in their country of origin.

Community organizing efforts can also be important vehicles for addressing the needs of immigrant communities and incorporating immigrants into civic life. Such efforts can provide the basis for achieving improved housing conditions, a living wage, better medical attention, and enhanced educational opportunities for all, and for empowering local communities. The United States Catholic Conference supports many such efforts through the Catholic Campaign for Human Development. The local church's participation in such efforts is important, both for the direct good that community organizing can do for individuals and groups and as part of a broader evangelization that proclaims God's care for all his children and the Church's special responsibility for the poor, the persecuted, and the stranger.

The call to solidarity is also a call to promote the effective recognition of the rights of immigrants and to overcome all discrimination based on race, culture, or religion. "It means

Solidarity with Migrant Farmworker Families

For more than ten years, Crossroads of Friendship/Caminos de Amistad, a cross-cultural youth program of the Diocese of New Ulm, has provided teens from local parishes in southern Minnesota the opportunity to live with individual migrant families in their homes in the Rio Grande Valley of southern Texas. Through the Office for Hispanic Ministry coordinated by Fr. Anthony Stubeda, the high school students prepare for eight months to experience daily life with their host families, attend school where they are a minority, and take a day trip across the border to Mexico. When they return to Minnesota, the students prepare presentations for their parishes and communities. Through Crossroads of Friendship/Caminos de Amistad, participants have become voices for new attitudes toward migrant workers, challenging misinformation and bringing more appreciation for the presence of Mexican American migrants in their communities.

bearing witness to a fraternal life based on the Gospel, which respects cultural differences and is open to sincere and trustful dialogue" (Pope Paul VI, *Octogesima Adveniens*, no. 17). Especially since World War II, the Church has devoted special efforts on behalf of the human rights of migrants and refugees throughout the world, and in the United States in particular. At the national level the U.S. bishops' Office of Migration and Refugee Services has addressed these issues through participation in public policy debates, special programs for refugees, and aid to dioceses. Diocesan officials and parish leaders often participate as well in city- or region-wide bodies aimed at gaining recognition for immigrants in local affairs and combating discrimination.

We Catholic bishops commit ourselves to continue to work at the national level to promote recognition of the human rights of all, regardless of their immigration status, and to advance fair and equitable legislation for refugees and prospective immigrants. Present efforts need to be strengthened and supported with new initiatives, both at the local level and at the national level as U.S. immigration law and practice change in the face of changing political pressures and social realities. In particular, Catholic lay people, diocesan officials, and bishops should continue to work together with community organizations, labor unions, and other religious bodies on behalf of the rights of immigrants in the workplace, schools, public services, our legal system, and all levels of government. The Catholic Church in the United States through the National Conference of Catholic Bishops, many of the state Catholic conferences, individual bishops, and other Catholic organizations have been meaningfully involved in social advocacy on behalf of migrant workers and other immigrants. We encourage others to place a higher priority on public social policies that impact this special population.

CONCLUSION: A CALL TO A NEW EVANGELIZATION

In *Ecclesia in America,* Pope John Paul II calls for a "new evangelization" centered on the person of Jesus Christ: "'The encounter with the living Jesus Christ' is 'the path to conversion, communion and solidarity'" (no. 7). This personal encounter with the risen Lord, so abundantly recounted in the Gospels, Epistles, and Acts of the Apostles, leads to a daily vision of the Lord present and active in the world, especially in the poor, in the stranger, and in the migrant and refugee. Those most in need draw the members of the Church out of their unawareness to a conversion of heart through which they are able to offer a genuine and suitable welcome, to share together as brothers and sisters at the same table, and to work side by side to improve the quality of life for society's most vulnerable members. All of this is an expression of the Spirit of the risen Jesus being poured out again on his followers.

The Holy Spirit made manifest at Pentecost enabled people of diverse languages and cultures to understand the one message of salvation. The new evangelization means openness to the gifts of the Spirit wherever they might appear. Our response to the new immigration thus is informed by a renewed vision of what it is to be Church, and by a new spirituality, informed by the Spirit of Pentecost present in the sacrament of confirmation, which gives the power to discern the one message of the kingdom in the diverse customs and languages of our immigrant brothers and sisters.

Immigrant communities give ample witness to what it is to be Church—in their desire to worship as a people, in their faith, in their solidarity with one another and with the weakest among them, in their devotion and their faithfulness to the Church of their ancestors. For the Church in the United States to walk in solidarity with newcomers to our country is to live out our catholicity as a Church. The Church of the twenty-first century will be, as it has always been, a Church of many cultures, languages and traditions, yet simultaneously one, as God is one—Father, Son, and Holy Spirit—unity in diversity.

The new immigration is a reminder of the pilgrim state of the Church, made up of all those, regardless of race or class or national origin, who have been called to the wedding banquet and have responded (Lk 14:23). As a pilgrim, the Church encompasses in itself all the reality of human suffering and all the glory of the human spirit infused with the grace of Christ. With its diverse pilgrim peoples, the Church in the United States has known uprootedness and loss, persecution and flight, the search for a better life, and the difficulties and disappointments of that search. The Church has known God's grace as it lifts spirits in times of despair, sustains hope in the face of hopelessness, and revives love despite evils and human frailties. In the one baptism, the Church acknowledges God's call to conversion, while in the sacrament of the Eucharist, she enjoys prefigured the glorious communion of Father and Son in the Holy Spirit. At the Eucharist the Church prefigures the revelation of "a great multitude . . . from every nation, race, people, and tongue" (Rev 7:9).

In such a Eucharist, on that sunlit Jubilee Day of Migrants and Refugees in St. Peter's Square, Pope John Paul II summed up the

*The Church of the twenty-first
century will be, as it has always
been, a Church of many cultures,
languages and traditions,
yet simultaneously one,
as God is one—
Father, Son, and Holy Spirit—
unity in diversity.*

challenge and hope for the Church in the United States as it welcomes the immigrants of the new millennium in a very simple but profound image:

> Like the disciples of Emmaus, believers, supported by the living presence of the risen Christ, become in turn the traveling companions of their brothers and sisters in trouble, offering them the word which rekindles hope in their hearts. With them they break the bread of friendship, brotherhood and mutual help. This is how to build the civilization of love. This is how to proclaim the hoped-for coming of the new heavens and the new earth to which we are heading. (no. 4)

NOTES

1. "In keeping with linguistic convention, the term Romani (also spelled Romany in the literature) is used to refer to any or all of the Romani dialects or languages. We use 'Gypsies' to refer to the totality of all groups except the Irish and Scottish Travelers, and where the identity of the group is unverified." (Taken from *Gypsies and Travelers in North America: An Annotated Bibliography*, William G. Lockwood and Sheila Salo [Cheverly, Md.: The Gypsy Lore Society, 1994].)

2. In international and U.S. law, "refugees" are those who have fled past persecution or have a well-founded fear of future persecution on account of race, religion, nationality, membership in a particular social group, or political opinion. While the United States may grant asylum or special consideration to some refugees, the process of obtaining such recognition is often fraught with difficulties, and many refugees must deal with the immigration system on the same terms as other immigrants.

3. Congress enacted three major laws in 1996 that have had an adverse impact on immigrants: (1) the Illegal Immigration Reform and Immigrant Responsibility Act (IIRIRA), (2) the Anti-Terrorism and Effective Death Penalty Act (AEDPA), and (3) the Personal Responsibility and Work Opportunity Reconciliation Act (PRWORA). Taken together, these laws have undermined due process protections for immigrants and driven more immigrant families into poverty. The combined effect of IIRIRA and AEDPA have subjected immigrants who committed minor crimes in their past and have served their sentence to mandatory detention and deportation, separating them indefinitely from their loved ones. IIRIRA also removed judicial discretion for individual cases and increased the standard for immigrants to obtain relief from deportation. It further included provisions that allow the summary exclusion of asylum seekers from this country without the benefit of review of their asylum claims by an immigration judge and bars immigrants who reside in the country in an

undocumented status for more than one year from returning to the United States for ten years. PRWORA, the federal welfare law, eliminated all legal immigrants from eligibility for public benefits. While some of these benefits have been restored, virtually all legal immigrants who entered the United States after 1996 remain ineligible for benefits.

4. Puerto Ricans, of course, are not immigrants, but many of them face the same challenges as recent immigrants. Much of the Hispanic population of the Southwestern United States, likewise, can trace its ancestry in what is now the United States back many years before the appropriation of these territories by the U.S. government. While having much in common in language and culture with recent immigrants, the Hispanos of New Mexico and many Mexican Americans throughout the country today welcome the newcomers in their midst as long-established residents of this country. At the same time, they have often experienced the discrimination and disadvantage associated with representing a subordinate culture in the United States, on a par with the experiences of recent immigrants.

5. The term "multicultural," like others surrounding the question of immigration, has been much disputed in the United States. Like "cultural pluralism," "multicultural" may describe a society in which multiple cultures exist peaceably side by side, interacting in common social, economic, and political practices, while remaining distinct in others; respecting one another; learning from one another; and each changing at its own pace accordingly. The call for "incorporation" articulated in this letter shares in this spirit. It is not a call for "assimilation" or the disappearance of one culture into another, but for continuing cooperation in pursuit of the common good and with proper respect for the good of each cultural tradition and community.

6. In February 1986 the Pontifical Commission for the Pastoral Care of Migrants and the Congregation for Catholic Education wrote a joint letter on the place of "Human Mobility in the Formation of Future Priests."